MAKE YOUR OWN
VOLCANO

BY MARI BOLTE

PEBBLE
a capstone imprint

Published by Pebble, an imprint of Capstone
1710 Roe Crest Drive, North Mankato, Minnesota 56003
capstonepub.com

Library of Congress Cataloging-in-Publication Data is available on the Library of Congress website.
ISBN: 9780756580858 (hardcover)
ISBN: 9780756580803 (paperback)
ISBN: 9780756580810 (ebook PDF)

Summary: Learn about chemical reactions with this easy and fun project. Gather some simple supplies, follow the steps, and sit back and watch what happens!

Editorial Credits
Editor: Erika L. Shores; Designer: Heidi Thompson; Media Researcher: Jo Miller; Production Specialist: Tori Abraham

Image Credits
Capstone: Karon Dubke: all project photos, supplies; Shutterstock: DanielFreyr, 5, Ivaschenko Roman, 20 (goggles), Noel V. Baebler, 21 (peroxide), NonTheerachai, 6 (water), Posteriori, 7 (salt)

Printed and bound in China. 5834

TABLE OF CONTENTS

Words in **BOLD** are in the glossary.

WHAT IS A VOLCANO?

Volcanoes are openings in Earth's surface. Some look like mountains. When they **erupt**, hot lava called **magma** explodes out the top.

Gather a few simple supplies to make your own volcano. It's a lot safer than a real one!

WHAT YOU NEED

- large bowl

- measuring cups and tablespoon

- spatula

- 1 cup (125 grams) flour

- 1/2 cup (63 g) table salt

- 1/2 cup (4 fluid ounces) warm water

- green and red food coloring

- 3-ounce paper cup

- baking tray

- 1 tablespoon (17 g) baking soda

- 1 tablespoon (15 milliliters) dish soap

- craft stick

- 1/2 cup white vinegar

WHAT YOU DO

STEP 1

In a large bowl, use the spatula
to mix the flour, salt, water, and
a few drops of green food coloring.
It should form a dough.

STEP 2

Roll the dough into a ball.

Set the paper cup in the center
of the baking tray.

STEP 3

Use the dough to shape a volcano around the paper cup.

Let the volcano dry overnight.

STEP 4

Pour the baking soda into the paper cup.

Add the dish soap to the baking soda.

Stir them together with the craft stick.

STEP 5

Pour the vinegar into a measuring cup.

Add a couple drops of red food coloring.
Stir them together.

STEP 6

Pour the vinegar mixture into the paper cup.

Watch what happens!

TAKE IT FURTHER

Make an even bigger eruption.
Ask an adult to help you.
Wear goggles for safety!

Replace the baking soda with
hydrogen peroxide. Replace the
vinegar with one packet of yeast
and 3 tablespoons (45 mL) of water.
Now watch your volcano erupt!

BEHIND THE SCIENCE

When vinegar and baking soda are mixed, they make a **gas** called **carbon dioxide**. This makes the mixture bubble over and the volcano erupt.

The dish soap helps the eruption last longer. It slows down the **chemical reaction**.

CARBON DIOXIDE

VINEGAR

BAKING SODA

GLOSSARY

carbon dioxide (KAHR-buhn dy-AHK-syd)—a gas with no color or smell

chemical reaction (KE-muh-kuhl re-ACK-shun)—a process in which one or more substances are made into a new substance or substances

erupt (ih-RUHPT)—to burst out suddenly with great force

gas (GAS)—a form of matter that is not solid or liquid; it can move about freely and does not have a definite shape

hydrogen peroxide (HYE-druh-juhn puh-RAHK-syd)—a liquid used to kill germs

magma (MAG-muh)—hot, molten rock beneath Earth's crust

ABOUT THE AUTHOR

Mari Bolte lives in the woods surrounded by books, animals, and crafting supplies. When she's not writing or editing books for kids, she's tromping through the woods looking for what's waiting to be discovered.